From The Inside Out
Spreading cheer

By Bro. James Earl Smith

From The Inside Out

Copyright, 2017 by James Earl Smith

ISBN-13: 978-1-944583-17-0

This book is published by Laurel Rose Publishing, 1930 Holston Rd, Como, MS 38619

TEL: 662-501-7129
E-MAIL: laurelrosepublishing@gmail.com
WEBSITE: www.laurelrosepublishing.com

Printed in the UNITED STATES OF AMERICA

Illustrations by: Summer Joor
Pictures by: Sandra Smith

Acknowledgement

This being my twelfth book; I continue to acknowledge the gift of the Holy Spirit that inspires me in my efforts to reach out to a troubled unstable world. With crimes on the rise and chaos erupting all across the globe, People need to hear a kind and comforting word from time to time.

Table of Contents

Part 1

Introduction to the Smith Family

Stretching out in many directions,
Our roots have spread over several
generations.
Starting out on a farm, we toiled in a
profession that seemed almost worthless,
Now our abilities are all but endless.
With the help of the Lord, we've made it
thus far.
And our next goal lies beyond the stars.
When our Lord returns to claim his own,
As he knows us, we will know him as he is
known.

The Smith Family

Robert, Lula, Robbie, Robert Earl, James Edward, James Earl, Lizzie, Lucille, Cubie, Doris, Katherine, Jimmy, Johnnie and Louise not pictured

Where There's Love There's Togetherness

*We are the Smith family; born and raised in the
heart of the south.*
*In our upbringing, our father was not without
merits*
And our mother was stern against all habits
But profanity found no place in her mouth.
Choosing God as her leader,
She became our counselor and teacher.
Showing obedience, we learned well
I trust all who read the words of this poem
Will heed the things I have to tell.
*Peas and corn bread, molasses and side meat,
these are delicacies not easy to forget*
But night pots and outdoor toilets, giving up, I
have no regrets.
Picking cotton, no one can say we didn't do a lot.
When it came time for work, we rallied together
like peas in a pot.
Togetherness gave strength to our family roots.
And love is the greatest asset of our family fruit.
It inspires the connecting genes in our hearts to
react
Keeping in contact with each other over the miles
helps to keep the bond intact.

We are a sharecropper' family who have had our
days in the sun
Though we shared much pain and sweat,
We even found time for fellowship and fun.
Our days were long; our nights were peaceful;
And with the support of each other
Our bellies were filled;
That gave us reasons to be cheerful and thankful.
With the cotton fields and mule plowing now all
behind,
We bear no shame of those bygone days.
Hauling water and slopping pigs: milking cows and
stripping sorghum: down on the farm
These we did, all with pride
But none of them gave us the incentive to stay.
We cleared little, whether we worked the fields of
Mr. Louis or Mr. Ray.
Neither of them gave us favorable pay.
Walking around with empty pockets
Like most black people, with this we were
accustom
But it wasn't something we chose by choice.
Now, as we reminisce our bygone days,
We embrace our upbringing without malice in our
voice.
Some near, some far away, we all now live
But through time and distant our love survives.

Lula Mae Redmon Smith was born August 1, 1928 in Lafayette County near Oxford, Mississippi to the Late Thelma Nelson Redmon and James Redmon. After her Mother and father separated, she and her five brothers were raised by their mother. She being the only girl among six siblings; she shared household and private home duties with her mother. At the age of eight, her childhood ended and she took on the responsibilities of a full grown adult in the corn and cotton fields as well as the cooking, washings, and cleaning of the family home. Juggling field and home chores left little time for play but it was the way of life for black children brought up on the farm. Money was scare so the families raised the majority of their food, made many of their own clothes, and made and repaired many of the items within their household. Children also learned how to make their own play toys. Lula was especially talented making rag dolls out of sticks and making clothes for them using whatever scrapped pieces of clothing she could find. At the age of fourteen, she married Robert Smith and to this union twelve children were born. Before marriage, Lula and her Husband, Robert, were both Mississippi born and brought up on the farm. Lula continued to do farm work for thirty eight years then left the field but continued to do the house chores of a farmer' wife for the next three years. In 1969, she moved to the town of Coldwater and got a job at the city' Record shop and worked there for eight years as a press operator. When the plant closed down, she went to the meat packing house in Hernando and worked for one year. In 1978 she landed a job at the Nursing Home in Senatobia, Ms. and worked for an additional 17 years. She retired from the Nursing Home in 1996 but continued to do private home work and baking for several more years. Her cakes and pies became loved across many states; people started calling her the cake lady. She loved cooking whether it was for hire or family and people loved stopping by to partake of her meals. During her life time she has been labeled with various names, among them "the Cake Lady" "Fabulous Hat wearing Lady", "Fancy Dressing Lady" and a "Lady of exceptional generosity." She is an extraordinary woman that has overcome many obstacles in her life. Amazingly, at the age of sixty, she acquired her driving licenses to drive a car. This not only gave her the ability to go where she wanted to; it also allowed her to hold down three jobs without depending on others for transportation. For years, public work, private home work, and bake sales, made up her daily schedule. This remarkable woman single handedly put her children through High school and college and continued to provide financial help, vegetables, jellies and jams, and counseling, to and for her children until her health failed.

Our Backbone (From Beginning to End)

Our mother, (**LULA),** has always been the family backbone.
Whether in birth, school, sickness, health, or work,
She has never left us alone.
It was she that kept us together and made sure we were fed
And on our journeys to the field each day, she led.
Like a shining beacon on the darkest night,
Before us, she was always our angel of light.
Guided by the spirit, she brought us up in the ways of the Lord
And she taught us ways that are honorable and right.
Many times through the shadow of death as she walked,
She carried hidden secrets of innumerable weight.
For the advancement of her children,
She labored with hands and feet.
None of our needs or goals did she hesitate to meet.
Her loving grace from others, she never turned.
In the sight of the one that dwells in the heaven of heavens,
A good name she has faithfully earned.
By her, her goodness and kindness have been shared with others.

But only we, her children, have shared her as a mother.
With a smile, each day, we watch her lay quietly in her bed.
Rarely a pain do she ever shed.
Above four scores and still within her right mind,
To us, she's a perfect example for all of womankind.
Except for the privilege of having her as our mom,
Nothing could make us more proud of what she has become.

Haiku of Lula

A stone of courage
Unbreakable by mistrust
Grounded in God' grace

Unbroken as yet
The strongest link in the chain
In forced by love

Our thoughts join with her'
We are part of each other
In many places

To God be glory
Faith nurtured us through the years
By your devotion

In midst of darkness
Through prayer you found God' grace
Salvation await

Robert Lee Smith (now 96 years old)

Born Robert Lee Smith to the late Frank and Lizzie Ward Smith in Senatobia Mississippi April 2, 1922, He was the third eldest of six siblings born to the couple. His education did not precede the second grade but it was enough to sustain his way of life. After losing his mother at the age of nine, he was placed in the care of his Mother eldest sister. Robert was a farmer from birth as his father before him and took on the profession as a career. Reaching the age of twenty-two, he felt he was ready to be the head of his own household. He married Lula Mae Redmon and together twelve children were born to their union. In February of 1944, just one month before their first child, Robbie, was born, Robert was drafted into the arm forces and served an honorable term of two years. After being dismissed from the army in 1946, he returned to the trade of his father. Returning home at the age of twenty-four, he took up the profession of farming by day while going to school at night studying mechanic for the next eighteen months. Sharecropping was a common profession of many families during the early ere of the twenty century so Robert adapted to it and raised his family up with it. During his years of farming, he progressed from sharecropper to tenant farmer but soon grew weary of both. After nearly five decades, in 1969, he left farm life behind, moved to Memphis Tennessee and became a truck driver working for the EZ storage moving company, for the next thirty years, he rode up and down the high ways from coast to coast delivering furniture. Feeling the need for rest, Robert retired from public work at the age of 90 and now lives alone in an apartment in Hernando Mississippi where he take pleasure in sharing with others who will listen the many adventures of his long blessed life. At the age of 96, his mind is still sharp and alert.

Pop! It took a little time to bring you around.
Hope always exists when you're above ground.
Above four scores and ten and still going strong,
Your time left is most likely shorter than long.
The desires of the flesh, the lust of the eyes, have
claimed many of men souls.
Many of your peers have gone on before you
But they found no permanent happiness in their
stroll.
You've seen things and been places some will
never see
But the thrill of them all cannot be compare to the
grace of a God that's able to set you free.
Many offspring bear your name.
Though, your relationship with them is not all the
same.
The good in life you sowed was far less than that
you've been given
But in time perhaps you'll be enlighten
God is good; God is gracious;
Like he does for all of us, he watches over you
night and day.
And even chasten you when you stray.
If you're faithful to him, he'll be faithful to you.
He offers you and all that believes the gift of his
slain Lamb
The blood of which makes your salvation sure.

Haiku of Robert

Throwing stone for stone
Regenerates the same guilt
Love dissolves faults

The conscience awakes
Guilt committed in the past
Faults are revived

By each lustful smile,
Evil is reborn again
Hell' fire lays in wait

Fears of fixation
Loneliness more apparent
Darkness ascends light

Nothing is hidden
Silent speaks even in death
Unknowns are made known

Cubie

Cubie with husband Edgar (7ᵗʰ Sibling)

Cubie Smith Joor was born October 12, 1953 in Coldwater Miss. Named by her uncle, Sam Reed, she still wonders after six decades where he got the name. She is the seventh of twelve siblings and the first of the siblings to graduate form an integrated school. Her first three years of high school was spent at Tate County High School as a Hawk and the last year of High School was spent at Coldwater High School as a Cougar. She graduated from Coldwater High School on May 1971 and worked at the Coldwater Record Plant for one year. Working at the Record Plant she learned that the work was similar to farm work with long hot hours and very little pay. Seeking an easier and better way of life, she decided to go to college. She entered Northwest Mississippi Junior College in Senatobia, MS. in 1972 and graduated with an Associate of Education degree in 1974. Transferring to Delta State University in Cleveland MS. she furthered her education and majored in Criminal Justice with a minor in Sociology. In December of 1976, she accomplished two great millstones in her life; she received her Bachelor of Science Degree in Criminal Justice from Delta State University and she entered into matrimony with Mr. Edgar Joor. She and Edgar received a Master of Education in counseling degree in May of 1979. The following year she worked in the Greenwood Public Schools System at Thread Gill Elementary School. From 1981-1989, she was employed with the Mississippi Library Commission in Jackson, Ms. and the latter end of 1989 she and her family moved to Daphne Alabama where in 1990 she landed a job with the University of South Alabama in Mobile, Al. and was there until 2011. She and her husband, Edgar, are now both retired and live in Richmond TX. The couple has two children and three grandchildren. She credits and gives God the glory and praises for his blessings of her family near and far.

Wandering Cubie

We've always called you Cubie
Yet I remember your first grade teacher
That insisted on calling you cubby.

With her opinion,
Being rear up in a family of humbleness,
You showed no disrespect or sign of bitterness.

I'm told when you were young, you hated your
name.
But it's a beautiful name and its pronunciation
carries no shame.

Arriving in Texas, you searched the web and found
your name to be one few others own.
This makes you special; in a state comprised of
millions of people, by the name Cubie, no others
are known.

You're like a wandering doe
Moving from place to place, always on the roam:
Venturing from Coldwater to Cleveland to
Jackson, Mobile, and finally to Texas
There you and Edgar have settled in your new
home.

The name Cubie was given you at birth
And you've honored the giver by proving your
worth.

You are the off spring of parents that came from
the roots of honorable dust
And you were brought up in a way of life that was
simple – but it was just.

Born on a farm, you were, yet the life style
thereof you chose not to take,
But the joys and sorrows of childhood days, none
of us can forsake.

From the days of old, you've come a long ways
And the lessons you learned alone the way were
what helped and shaped you into the great
mother, loving wife, and adorable sister that you
are today.

You are one of six sisters that share the same
blood line with six brothers.
We all are the off spring of the same father
But our greatest possessions, charity, honor,
mercy, humility, and perseverance, we owe to our
mother.

Haiku of Cubie

A three state dweller
Leaving love from state to state
Mississippi born

True love never dies
By your mother' example
Your family thrives

Carrying for your own
With a love from home,
A soul in cow girl country

Keeping faith alive
Though the road gets rough and long
Service continues

Caught up in between
Where love and devotion fail
Harmony cries out

Katherine, Cat, Kitty Kat, Kitty Rat, (9th Sibling)

Katherine Smith

Katherine Smith, short for Kat, and nick named Kitty Rat, is the ninth child and youngest girl born to Robert Lee and Lula Mae Smith. She was born 1957 and attended Central Tate Elementary, Tate County High School, and Coldwater High School where she graduated in May of 1974. During the summer months of 1974 she worked for the Record Factory in Coldwater as a Record Inspector and went on to attend Northwest Junior College in the fall of that same year. Her major was secretary science. In the fall of 1976 she transferred to Delta State University in Cleveland, Mississippi where she majored in Business Administration. While at DSU, she was crowned queen of the Black Student's Union Ball in 1977 and in 1979 she went on to receive a Bachelor of Business Administration Degree from DSU and moved to Detroit, MI. seeking employment. From 1979-2001, she worked for a law firm in Southfield, MI. with a title of Secretary/book keeper/Property Manager. From 2002-2005 she worked as a Manager for McDonald. Kat was a member of the ban of flutes when she attended Central Tate Elementary school. She is now single and has one daughter, two granddaughters and one grandson. Looking back over her life she renaissance life on the farm with all her siblings. She acknowledges and gives God the credit for giving her and her siblings the strength to keep pressing on toward higher callings in spite of the hardships they were faced with in the days of their youth. Katherine now lives in Oak Park, MI. and attends the First Baptist Church of Oak Park in Oak Park MI. She further thanks God for where he has brought her from and for how he is still blessing her now.

Curious Kat

For short, the family calls you Kat.
And sometimes little sister, you may even hear me call you kitty rat.
You grew up with bigger brothers and sisters to look up too
And they became champions in your view.
Like Ba Dear, you make a superb peach pie.
It's a delicacy from you in which I can always rely
You are a member of the Smith' clan
And to each other from time to time we must lend a helping hand.
With the heart of a lioness in providing for motherly needs,
Your love and concerns are displayed in deeds.
When we were children, these days were not foreseen.
We know not what tomorrow holds but we know what all of our yesterdays have been.
Like a cat, you're curious and playful
But as a sister you're lovable and delightful.
From Coldwater to Cleveland, you once took a hike.

With your hair flowing in the wind, your body was motionless on the back of a bike.
If Chatty Cathy was here today, would you hold her as dear as you did in your youth?
So many memories we've left in the past yet they're undeniable truths.
The relationship between sisters and brothers should never grow stale.
And thanks to the proper upbringing of our parents
Neither of us has ever been in jail.
Kat, your sense of duty inspires emotions
And - you're a sister deserving of all our devotion.

Haiku of Cat

Faithful traveler
Doing your share in service
Others benefit

When parents are down
And helping hands are needed
Your' are known to serve

Duty earns its crown
Age carries no advantage
Heaven knows your work

To soothe the conscience
Excuses are ever made
Love keeps on going

Doris (8th Sibling)

Doris Day Smith Davis is the 8th child of Robert Lee and Lula Mae Redmon Smith born February 20, 1955. She is the 8th of twelve siblings and 6th of the Smith siblings to graduate from high School as an honor student. Doris graduated from Coldwater High School in 1973; she was a member of the Beta Club, Drama Club, FBLA, (Future Business Leaders of America) and was considered "teacher's pet" because of her penmanship. She left Coldwater in 1973 and moved to Detroit, Michigan where she rejoined her high school sweetheart, Nathaniel Davis, and the following year on February 25th 1974 the two were married at the city county building in Detroit and to their union four children were born. She got a job as soon as she got to Detroit at a dry cleaner not realizing that that job would become a passion of her'. At the request of her husband, she became a stay at home mom to raise their children while they were young and he became the sole bread winner of the family. After about eight years, she returned back to work in the dry cleaning profession and has continued in the same profession for 35 years. Sadly in March of 1992, unexpectedly, she lost her husband and she became the sole bread winner for her four children so in addition to her full time job she took on a part time job cleaning buildings to help ends meet. Today, her children are all grown and have families of their own but Doris is still working at the dry cleaner and loving every minute of it. In addition to her four children, she now has seven grandchildren and loves spending quality time with them. From her childhood, Doris has loved the hobbies of sewing and cooking. She still get a joy out of cooking and has added to that joy attending church, singing with her church group and traveling back down home to Mississippi from time to time to visit family and friends. Doris has not yet retired but it's in her future plans to do so and travel to Hawaii. Though Doris only saw the latter part of her family farm life, she seemed to have had a magic touch for getting things her sisters were not able to get. As she thanks God for her family; her family thanks God for her.

Mysterious Doris

You were named after a movie star.
A star you're not but a Smith Sibling you truly are.

Even though, your big sister gave you the name
Doris Day,
I'm clueless as to why we call you Day Day.

Though you're grown up now, we still refer to you
by that name.
A daughter, a wife, a mother, and widow, all
these, you can also acclaim.

They say you were papa' pick down on the farm
And the weakness in his heart that led to his
pockets you knew how to charm.

I'm told there were times when your sisters had
no money for lunch
But you had enough to feed a bunch.

Who would have thought the little girl we called
meat
Would have had the ability to be so discreet:

Recalling the days of our childhood pranks
From what we were to what we are today, we
owe God the thanks.

Our little sister, Day Day, that skipped and hopped
across the bear' tail
One day grew into a woman and became a big city
gale.

Haiku of Doris

In your days of youth,
You had your day in the sun
Dad was your softy

Life carries a price
There's a debt we all owe
Those we leave behind

While the sun still shines
Whatever you do in life
Remember your roots

Fun we all desires
Love should supersede pleasures
Duty heals regrets

James Edward (3rd Sibling) with wife Lucy

James Edward Smith is the third child of Robert and Lula Smith born March 28, 1948 in the community of Arkabutla Mississippi. Like all his siblings, he was farm born and farm raised; he found contentment as a child fighting bees, rolling tires, playing balls, and having the skill to create and make play toys like pole horses, top shooters, bow and arrows, sling shots, and kites. He found farm life to be hard but tolerable. Leaving high school in 1966, he went to Detroit, Michigan seeking a different way of life. Within that same year, he married Lucy Ann Boyd and started his new career on the assembling line at Chrysler Corporation. A few days working at Chrysler made him realize that farm work was not as bad as he thought it was when he compared it to the assembling line but the inner strength that was within him, thanks to the great up bringing he had received from home, church and school, gave him the perseverance to face the challenge. During his stay at Chrysler, he worked at different levels starting from the assembling line to Repairman to Quality Control Inspector to Engine Repairman to Major Repairman. Acquiring his GED in 1967, he went on to attend several different learning institutions to better his status at Chrysler. In 1968, he attended Wolverine trade school, in 1969, Motech Automotive School, in 1970, Highland Parks Community College and in 1971, Henry Ford's Community College and also Randolph Phillip's Carpenter School. As he moved up the Corporate ladder, the Company continued to send him back to school at their expense which gave him the knowledge and credentials to achieve the job of his dream in 1992 (he was set up in the engineering department). James worked for Chrysler for 41 years. Since the start of his manhood in 1966, he has managed to keep busy; he started a mechanic side business at his home in1969, became an ordained Deacon at his church in

1972, joined with his brother in-laws in 2009 and acquired a rental property business. Today, James is the father of four children and 14 grandchildren. For a man that left home at the age of eighteen with nothing but a dream desiring to be a TV repairman, he has had a busy, but successful life.

Haiku of James Edward

Finding thrill in much
Coupled with fascination
Joy is expressed

Mississippi love
On the streets of Detroit
Carrying the Smith' torch

Brother James

You were always the adventurous one, always having an urge to go
As you grew older, that urge continued to grow.

Many times I desired and wished to be as you
But the things you did I was always too shy to do.

Those times we spent together swinging on vines
and trees
Those heroic days again we will never see.

In the mornings, we rose to milk the cows
And from sun up to sun down in the spring time,
our times were spent behind the plow.

We'll always carry in our memory old jack and old
crow
Bits and pieces of those days we'll never outgrow.

The life of a farmer was not our dream
But sweat and pains were in our regime.

Recalling the time you took a snake into the house
to frighten Ba Dear;
I remember her hollering
And toward your head her six- shooter was
aiming.
With death lurking on your heels,
You and your shadow were franticly running.
And believe me brother
Your feet weren't stalling.

Around the television set each night
We watched westerns like Roy Rodger and the
Cisco Kid.
After the sun went down

With nothing else to do
This is what we did.

Thinking back on those days of yester-year
There're so many things we hold so dear.

Things like our first picnic on the 4th of July
And all the mysteries of youth now gone by

What I could only do with the use of pen and
paper
With word of mouth you mastered the caper.
You're a farm boy from a southern town;
You left the cotton sack and you left the hoe
And headed north in search of progress.
Like a wise old geese, you took your flight into
uncharted territories and became a success.
By your side, Lucy stood faithfully urging you on.
And no obstacle did you ever have to face alone.
With only a dream to claim as a memento,
You entered mechanic school not knowing a thing
And now I'm told you're the city' pro.

Making a home in a new found land
You paced the way for the family to expand

When our siblings set foot on their new frontier,
It was good to know they had a big brother like
you near.

Jimmy Smith (11th Sibling)

Jimmy Smith with wife Mary

Jimmy Lee Smith, the eleventh child of Robert Lee and Lula Mae Smith, was born December 1, 1959 in Coldwater Mississippi. He attended and graduated from the Coldwater High School in 1977. During the summer of 1977 he participated in the "Upper Bound Program" and attended Rust College in Holly Springs, Mississippi. During the fall of 1977, he enrolled at Mississippi Valley State

University in Itta Bena, Ms. and graduated in 1981 with a Bachelor of Science Degree in Criminal Justice. With jobs very scare, during the summer of 1981, he did a number of odd jobs (assisting with building cabinets, carpentry, appliance parts runner, and working long hours at the Coldwater's Cotton Gin. In February 1982, he enlisted in the U.S. Navy as a E-3 in the field of Cryptology as a Cryptologist Technician and received basic training (aka Booth Camp) in Orlando, Florida. Upon completion of basic training in April 1982, he transferred to Pensacola, Florida for training to become a Manual Morse Code Operator. He transferred from Pensacola in September 1982 to his first Navy assignment at Naval Security Group Activity (NSGA) Sabana Seca, Puerto Rico. It was here where he met up with his wife to be (Mary) who was also in the navy. His next transfer was to NSGA Pyongtaek, South Korea in January of 1985. While stationed there, he was able to fly over and visit Japan. In early 1986, after completing Direct Support Training (afloat related), in Pensacola, he transferred to the U.S. Flag Ship "USS La Salle" (AGF-3) for a one year tour in the Middle East. During that one year tour, equal time (3 months each) was split between the USS La Salle, USS O'Bannon (DD-450), USS Luce (DDG-38), and USS Nicholson (DD-982). While assigned to the aforementioned Navy Ships, port visits were made in Karachi, Pakistan, Bahrain, Saudi Arabia, Oman, United Arab Emirates, and Djibouti (located in the Horn of Africa). His most memorable moment while stationed in the area was his transit in the Red Sea. He remembers looking across the mass body of water and imagining how Moses must have felt leading the children of Israel across the Red Sea on dry land. Upon leaving the Middle East in January of 1987, that same year in May, he married Mary Burney of Chattanooga, Tennessee and in August of that year he

received military training at Good Fellow Air Force Base (GAFB), in San Angelo, Texas. After his training, he and Mary received assignments to Oahu, Hawaii. He was assigned at NSGA Kunia. Upon departing Hawaii in 1991, he received additional training at GAFB. Upon completing training there, he was transferred to the National Security Agency (NSA) at Ft Meade, Md. Upon leaving Maryland in1995, he was transferred to the USS Thomas S. Gates (CG 51) in Norfolk, Va. During his tenure onboard, his six month Mediterranean Cruise took him to ports in Barcelona Spain, to Italy, where he saw the leaning Tower of Pisa, France, and to Rome, where he visited the ruin of the famous Roman Coliseum and the Papal Basilica of St. Peter Cathedral in the Vatican City within the city of Rome; Istanbul, Turkey (where he visited the Grand Bazaar which is one of the largest and oldest covered trade markets in the world, Greece, Romania where he observed the famous "Rock of Gibraltar" located near the Southwestern tip of Europe. After returning from the Mediterranean Cruise, he eventually headed down to Panama where he became a "Shellback' (Nickname given to sailors who had crossed the equator). Other than the various countries visited, his most memorable moment occurred when he received his Enlisted Surface Warfare (SW) specialist insignia (aka ESWS Pin—which signify minimum basic knowledge of
every departments of assigned ship) he was assigned a second tour at NSA from 1998-2000; from 2001-2002, he served as NSGA Ft. Meade Command Physical Fitness Coordinator for over 1300 Navy personnel assigned to both NSA and NSGA FT. Meade. One of his memorable moments at NSA was being selected/ promoted to Chief (SW) Cryptologist Technician. He retired in February 2002 with 20 years of dedicated service in the U. S. Navy. Since

retiring from the Navy, he has been employed with the Department of defense within the Washington/ Maryland/D.C. Area (aka DMV) and resides in Triangle, Va. with his wife, Mary, of 30 years. They have one son, four grandchildren and two great grandchildren. Jimmy and his wife, Mary, make regular visits to Tennessee and Mississippi on a yearly basic to visit with family and friends.

Little Brother Jim

Though young you were when you lost your finger,
Not a tear from your eyes did you shed in fear or anger.
Before you left home, you became a man
And set your sights on foreign lands.
You entered the navy to make a career
And you became like a modern day buccaneer.
Secrets you were bound by creed to keep.
Up and down the oceans, you and your companions made many sweeps.
You visited France and Hawaii too
And mighty whales you were blessed to see within your view.

Surrounded by more water than a man could drank
Many of meals you ate sitting in a steal tank.
Each time you and your comrades came in the presence of foreign soil,
I'm sure there were times you burned the midnight oil.
Twenty years you devoted your service to Uncle Sam
But your life was devoted to the spiritual Lamb.
When it came time to choose a life between land and sea,
You chose land as the place you preferred to be.
With you and Mary both being navy vets,
You each have the right to ride in a navy jet.
Remembering the days of your youth
I'm reminded of two undeniable truths.
1. You never had the privilege of baking a pig's melt.
2. Picking two hundred pounds of cotton, you never knew how it felt.
But you were given the privilege of being our baby brother
And with that in mind, telling you of your heroics and our forever gracefulness, I need not go any further.

Jimmy' Haiku

Uncle Sam' agent
Twenty years on land and sea
Keeping an eye out

Between sea and sky
More water than man can drink
Riding alone smooth

Bound by creed and rules
Representing the U.S
Your duty was clear

Back on solid grounds
At bay the enemy looks on
Peace is still in doubt

Lucille and Husband Orlando (6th Sibling)

Lucille Smith Davis was born July 10, 1952 in Coldwater Mississippi. She is the sixth sibling in a family of twelve. She graduated in 1970 as class valedictorian of her senior class from the Tate County High School and was the last of her siblings to graduate before integration. From 1970-1972, she attended Northwest Junior College and in 1972 she entered into matrimony with her high school sweetheart, Orlando Davis. The next eighteen months of her life was spent in Colorado Springs Colorado where Orlando was stationed during his term of enlistment. After Orlando discharge, they moved to Memphis Tennessee and made it their home. From 1975-1984, she worked as a teacher at Southside Kinder garden. From 1984-1991, she was a stay-at-home mom. For the next eighteen years, she worked at Raines Haven Elementary as a special need teacher. She then went on to Fairley High School and for the next seven years worked in the Resource Department from 2008-2014. After four decades of teaching other people children and caring for her own four sons and a number of grandchildren on the side, she retired from the Memphis City School System in May of 2014 and now devotes most of her time as a caregiver for her mom. She credits her success in life to the many fond memories of her childhood days spent on the farm with her mother and father and all her siblings working and playing together in harmony. If there was one thing the entire Smith family learned, it was how to endure hardships. Those lessons she learned have served as companions of strength on many occasions in her life. Her philosophy in life, she says is, through all the trials and tribulations I may have encountered over the years, I still remember the words of the apostle Paul who said "I can do all things through Christ who strengthen me." (Philippians 4:13)

Faithful Lucille

Your parents and siblings all call you Cile
But all of your friends call you Lucille.

As a child, your head was always face to face with
the pages of a book.
The thirst for knowledge you never forsook.

Like your elder siblings, you were introduced to
work while you lived on the farm.
Hard work and constant studying molded you into
the profession of a caring schoolmarm.

I don't remember the humps Cubie packed within
your cotton sack
But I imagine they resembled the humps on a
camel' back

Down on the farm when we all were together
There was closeness we shared one with the
other.

The days of yesteryear may have all passed on by
But as long as there're memories, they'll always
be nigh.

During your teenage years your short dresses and
knees you loved to show

But when you joined up with Orlando your dresses came down and your knees were covered because what he saw of you he wanted no other boys to know.

And there was that special hairdo you loved that no one but Cubie knew how to fix.
Things we did or loved in the past, today many of them seem like fiddlesticks.

But with the important things in life we learn to immerse.
Perhaps it's why you went to college to become a nurse:

That healing spirit Ba Dear and Mom Ma, saw in you
Others are inspired by it also, when you're in their view.
Be assured God knows all that you're doing and have done.
Family and friends have also witnessed your phenomenon.
The devotion you've given to Ba Dear
Cannot be measured or weighed.
It's far more than a helping hand you've given
You've kept your word just as you promised.

Haiku of Lucille

A promise keeper
Kindness and mercy are shown
Covering your deeds

Easy to panic;
In service, unwavering;
Bound by charity:

Though the road gets rough
Devotion never weakens
A spirit of love

Maintaining service
Relief is a rarity
Service is a must

The duty of love
Magnifies the Lord' presence
Witnessed by works

On call day and night
Going in and out of sleep
The watch continues

Johnnie (10th Sibling)

Johnnie Smith is the tenth child of Robert Lee and Lula Mae Smith. He was born on a farm in Coldwater Mississippi on March 2, 1958. He went on to graduate from the Coldwater High School in May of 1976. Immediately after High School, he landed a job as a part time Roofer at a starting fee of $5.00 per hour. His first full times job was at the Baddour Center in Memphis Tennessee where he worked for seven months before moving on in 1977 to AMAC, a company that specialized in aluminum, for another seven months. Then, from August 1977 to May of 1979, he found himself unemployed. Luckily in June of 1979, he was employed under the Cedar Program for the Senatobia Housing Authority for two years. By 1981, wedding bells were ringing and he joined in union with Jenett Newsom, a marriage that lasted for only two years. However, within those two years, the couple had two daughters, (one since has deceased) before separation. In 1981, Johnnie also became employed at one of his favorite site, the Hernando Packing House, where he worked for about 14 years. It was about that time, 1981, when he started his detailing profession too. The first car he detailed was his own, a 1983 Buick Century but the first car he detailed for hire was a Park Avenue owned by Samuel Davis of Coldwater, Ms. for a fee of $10.00. After the Packing House closed, Johnnie went to Atlas Doors in Nesbit Ms. and worked until they closed down. In 1997 a terrifying accident opened up the eyes and heart of Johnnie while he was on his way to work; his car hydro planed and flipped five times and plunged into a 20 feet deep gutter. While he was upside down with water constantly running in, it was then that he called upon the God that his mother had leaned and depended on all of her life. Johnnie said that God heard and answered his prayer but what he failed to realize was that God was right there when he had the accident. In diver ways and at diver times, God gets our attention and causes us to acknowledge his presence and saving power. It was in 1998 that Johnnie chose the name "Mr. Detail" and many know and call him by that name today. Johnnie worked for the town of Coldwater from 2003 to 2004 then the Hernando Packing House relocated to Oakland, Ms. and Johnnie was hired and worked for four months before the government closed it down. Returning back to Coldwater, Johnnie started working for the city of Senatobia in various positions and has been employed thus far for 13 years. Johnnie has four grandchildren and has worked more different jobs to date than any of his Siblings before or after him.

Johnnie Cool

With Jimmy and Bo Willie, you grew up as a team of three.
Whatever the bond that held the relationship together
Adulthood seems to have caused it to flee.

I know Johnny Smith is your given name
And I've heard that in school basketball was your game.

At some point in life, you started calling yourself Johnny Cool.
At that time, your skill at chess demonstrated that the mind is an awesome tool.

Today, you prefer to be called Mr. Detail.
The greatest detailer in town whose product is not for sale:

You're not the easiest person to find.

Unpredictable as a straight line wind;

Trying to reach you is a difficult task;
Your number changes like AT&T.
By way of Texas seems our best route
But that's not always a guarantee.
Into your own reality, you've taken a journey like
the prodigal son.
Back into the family circle, we hope you return
before the setting of life final sun.

Haiku of Johnny

Nick named poor boy
Before Detail you were Cool
Now a missing link

In and out again
A sibling verily seen
One heard through Texas

Home, you will not stay
Dropping in unannounced
Left-overs vanish

A son: a brother:
Devotion of a stranger
A rare encounter

Etta Robbie Mae Smith
Renfroe (1st Sibling)

Etta Robbie Mae Smith was born to the parents of Robert
Lee and Lula Mae Smith on March 3, 1944. Given the name
Etta after the famed singer, Etta James, for years, disliking
the name, she refused to use it but in later years she
embraced it and today prefers that people call her by it.
She is the eldest of twelve siblings; the first to start school

and first to marry, the first to leave home and start a family of her own. Robbie left school and got married to Hugh Renfroe on October 30, 1962 after reaching the ninth grade. For the next few years, they moved about from place to place but eventually separated. Robbie was left to raise her children on her own. She got her first public job around 1971 at the Coldwater Record Factory where she worked until she was laid off in 1972.

After getting laid off, she left her five eldest children with her mother in Coldwater and she and her youngest two children caught a bus and headed to Detroit Michigan in search of a better life for her family. After about a month, she got a job through the Michigan Employment Office after paying a fee of $25.00. Her first Michigan job was at a Grill owned by Willie Tippet who taught her how to short order cook.

With the skills learned from Willie Tippet, her qualification helped her to land a job in the Michigan School System in 1973 where she continued to work in various positions for the next thirty-five years before she retired in 2008. Moving back to Mississippi in 2009, she came out of retirement for 18 months and worked for a city day care center. When she lived as a care giver in the home of her mother, she observed all of her siblings graduation pictures on her mother' wall, it was then she decided to take the steps in 2009 to secure her diploma and now her picture hangs on the wall beside her Siblings pictures. After a three year stay in her native home of Mississippi, she had a yearning to return to the northern life of the big city. In June of 2010, she returned back to Michigan and made her home in Redford Michigan where she now dwells retired from public work but she continues to urge and counsel her children, grandchildren, and all who values her knowledge, in ways that are just and honorable before man and God.

Etta Robbie (Our Big Sis.)

Born in the wake of world war two
With no clue of the things that was going on around you.
You were first born and eldest among us
And as our big sister, you're a plus.
I understand you have a love for cooking
But many who know you have a greater love for eating.
Perhaps we don't talk as much as we ought too
And certainly we don't get together as often as we need too.
If a person could attain all the goals in life he/she pursues,
Nothing would be greater than having a sister like you.
In you resides the bulk of the family history
Deep down locked away, it's somewhere in your memory.
You may remember the snake in the corner of the ceiling you saw when we lived on the Slocum place.

But I bet you don't remember the expression you
had on your face?
Do you remember the hill side bank where we
attained eatable dirt?
We ate our fill and it never caused hurt.
The past holds both joys and miseries
Things we still retain in our memories.
Though we all live in separate places
The love we share should keep us close.
Sibling relationships should never seem comatose.
Whether we're together or apart from one
another,
Let's always pray one for the other.

Haiku of Robbie

Beginning the roots
A total of twelve in all
None can claim your place

A Skill for baking
Daughter, Sister, mother, wife
Service never ends

From out of darkness
In midst of a mother' love
Untouched by war

Still within God' grace
Facing three scores and thirteen
Thankful for so much

Robert Earl with Wife Rosie (2nd Sibling)

Robert Earl Smith, the second child and oldest son of Robert Lee Smith and Lula Mae Redmon Smith was born on Feb. 5, 1947 in the community of Arkabutla Mississippi. He was an organizer and lead taker. He organized the family' first family reunion in 1982; he was the first, along with his brother James Earl, of the family to graduate from high School, the first of his eleven siblings to drive an automobile, the first of the siblings to own a car and gun, first to attend and graduate from college, the first to teach school, and the first of his siblings to teach Sunday school and bible class. He attended and graduated from the Tate County high school as an honor student in May of 1967. He went on to attend North West Junior College in the fall of that same year. Furthering his education, he transferred to Delta State University and went on to receive a Bachelor of Science Degree in Social Studies and a Master Degree from Mississippi State University, in Starkville Mississippi. He also did further studies at the University of Southern Mississippi in Hattiesburg, Mississippi. He was a member of the Mississippi Association of Educators, the National Association and Holly Springs Association of Educators. He loved and was a football coach at Holly Springs High School and was a teacher for a total of twenty-three years combined between Itta Bena High School in Itta Bena, Mississippi and Holly Springs High School in Holly Springs Mississippi. He married Rosie Marie Jackson on August 1, 1971 and they were blessed with three children to their union. One of his greatest loves in life was teaching others, in all walks of life, the words and love of our risen Lord whether it was on Sunday morning in Sunday school or during his outreach and prison ministry. He was a dedicated God driven man.

What A Man

(A poetic picture of Mr. Robert E. Smith)

Born the son of a sharecropper,
This nobody in the eyes of society,
He was elevated to a stature of greatness.
Accepting his call at an early age,
He became a modern day John the Baptist in spirit
and goodness.
Proudly displaying the family's birthmark (a gentle
smile),
He became a drum major for faith and a man
among men.
What a man this was;
He fought a continuing spiritual battle against the
wages of sin.
Those who were blessed with the opportunity to
know him, to walk with him, and talk with him
Will always remember him as the dutiful teacher
that walked within their presence
The things he taught in words and deeds
We will treasure in our hearts till the end of our
days
Remembering this faithful man with his friendly
smile
That the saints of God will surely miss.
This man who refused to stop, knew not how to
quit

But continued to run the race of faith with patience
Knowing his crown and Lord stood waiting at the end.
Every confrontation made him stronger; every victory gave him courage;
When he was talked about, lied on, and called everything but a child of God,
This man, like Jesus, showed no malice or ill feelings toward his offenders
But daily he went down on his knees and prayed for his enemy as well as his friend.
This man with his continuing smile
Was accompanied by the shield of faith and the sword of the spirit wherever in life he went;
As an ambassador for Christ, he devoted himself to the service of the Lord
And his life and works spoke out so boldly
Neither saint nor sinner can ever deny
This man truly by God was sent.
Many homes were stunned one dreadful Thursday evening
In April of nineteen hundred and ninety-four,
When it was said that Robert had been taken from among us,
Tears ran down like rivers of waters
And hearts were filled with grief and sorrow for this man of God
That in service gave of his best.

This faithful man who stirred up the spirit of God
In men and women wherever he went
God called him on home to take his rest.
What a man this was that fought many battles for
the cause of righteousness,
He was one that showed no fear of the devil or
men.
Today this mighty warrior's body is confined to
the realm of his grave
BUT
Robert E. Smith and his works will never be
forgotten.

Haiku of Robert Earl

Some roots never die
Through the love of family
Life continues on

Out spoken, fearless
Driven by dedication
Talk backed by walk

Absence in the flesh
As long as family lives
Memories survive

On us down below
From the heaven of heavens
Your spirit looks on

Louise Smith Conley

Louise is the grandchild that grew up in the home with the 12 Smith Siblings. She too is a Smith and the oldest among her siblings of 12

Louise Smith Conley is the daughter of Etta Robbie Mae Smith and Ira Simmons. She is not one of the twelve Smith siblings but she is the only grandchild of Robert and Lula Smith that was born and raised in their home alongside of their own children. Louise was born July 13th 1961 in Coldwater, Mississippi while the family lived on the Slocum farm. She, herself, is also the twelfth sibling in a family of twelve. Raised by her grandmother until she was twelve, she was sent to Detroit, Michigan to live and help her mother with her other siblings. Moving about from place to place, Louise attended several different schools in Mississippi and Michigan before graduating from Redford High School in Michigan in 1980. She got her start working in the cotton field picking cotton while pulling a croaker sack while sometime riding on the back of her Aunt Lizzie' sack. She also made pocket change at various other jobs like dancing, babysitting, and private home work, City Street cleaning, worked at a Movie Theater and as noon hour aide at Brighmoor Elementary. She worked from 1979 to 1983 on part time and full time jobs and was able to move out on her own. In July of 1983 she moved to Killeen, Texas and was married within the same month to Louis Conley in Belton Texas. Leaving Texas in December of 1983, she moved back to Coldwater and stayed with her grandmother Lula, again until July of 1984. After which, she moved to Augsburg Germany and worked both as a waitress and waitress supervisor; she also ran the Office Club, NCO Club, enlisted men Club, formal party area and slot machines. When her second child was born, she worked as a volunteer in the baby ward at Augsburg Hospital and also got her driver licenses in 1985. Before leaving Germany, she was privileged to visit Paris France and Italy. In 1987 she moved back to Coldwater and stayed with her grandmother until her husband found housing for them in Leesville, La. While stationed at Fort Polk, La. Louise again worked as a waitress and at a Nursing Home. In 1989, she again returned to her grandmother' home in Coldwater and got a job as a Nurses' Aide at Senatobia Convalescent home and also worked at UPS and a Mom and Pop restaurant. While living within their own house on 107 West Street in Senatobia, her fourth and final child was born. She started working at Walmart in June of 1994 and has been there for 23 years. Divorcing in 1994, she and her children moved to two different homes before she bought the home which she now lives in and continued to work part time jobs at Aluminum Extrusion , Fred' dollar store, and private home work. Continuing her education, she received an Associate of Applied Science Degree in Child Development and Technology in 1997 and an Associate of Arts Degree in Physical Education/Recreation in 2000. Today while working as a part time care worker at her grandmother' house, she also holds down a full time job as an overnight support manager at Walmart. In addition to her four children, Louise has three grandchildren and welcomes God' blessings each and every day.

Spirited Louise

Your given name is Louise
Though some people may call you Wee-se
And others have a tendency of calling you Easy.

Your heritage is linked to the educated Smith clan.
A family known for their knowledge, good will, and
personality,
But for their singing ability, they seem to have few fans.

The Smith blood line can be traced back to your birth
So it's only natural that you should look like one.
You're a part of a family that embraces each day with
orison.

Rear up with five Aunts who were like sisters to you;
You were their pride and joy because you were littler.
As you all grew up and moved from place to place,
You were the only one that once lived in the land of
Adolph Hitler.

Reminiscence a few memory blasts;
I'm reminded of several episodes of the past.

Your skill in picking cotton were never one of fame
But with you and your croaker sack others often played
games.

And, there was that time you and your brother were sent
across the pasture to fetch water
And you stopped to moo' and moo' a bull with continuous
blaster.

But when the bull decided to challenge your mockery,
You threw down your water bucket and showed who was
faster.

Crossing the expressway between your mother and
grandmother' homes,
You were always the one out front.
And I know you'll never forget the day you stopped to take
a break,
Unaware, you invaded the ground of chiggers on the hunt.

I recall the time I thought Ex-lax was chocolate candy
But you, I'm told, once chewed into a chunk of lye soap
thinking it was coconut.
Looking back on the mysteries of our childhood days
They were more exciting than Gulliver's travels to Lilliput.

Today, whether you're living here or abroad,
Never forget that you're one of us.
Nothing surrounding your heritage could ever be
considered a cuss.

James Earl With Wife Gloria (4th Sibling)

James Earl Smith is the fourth sibling in a family of twelve. I was born March 30, 1949 in the small community of Arkabutla Mississippi. I graduated from the Tate County High School in 1967; one of eleven honor students out of one hundred and twenty plus students. I started night school in 1989 and graduated from Northwest community College in Senatobia Mississippi as the post child for that year with an Associate of Arts degree in 1994. Retiring after forty-four years working in a furniture warehouse I devoted my time to writing and hobbies. I also have a number of diplomas and certificates attained through many hours and years of home study courses. They include a diploma from World Bible School, one from Carver Bible College, one from Caldwell College; certificates are from the Carvel Sunday school hour, The PTL club, Lamp light studies, and studies from Ambassador College under the late Herbert W, Armstrong. I am a life time member of the International Society of Poets, a member of the ANA with more than four decades in the study of numismatics, an author with one book detailing by family' history, a poet with seven poetry books published thus far, a play writer with one book published thus far, a religious writer with two books to my credit thus far and have constructed hundreds' of cross word bible puzzles for various home study classes. I am also a deacon in the Baptist church, Sunday School Superintendent, and a Sunday school teacher of thirty-nine years. With several hobbies to my credit, through the blessings of God I've been successful in acquiring a number of trades. Married with four children; I'm a country born, country raised, and country loved child of God who's determined to draw others to the God that has been my guide from the days of my youth to this present day. I can do all things through Him as long as I believe and trust in Him.

Shy Earl

Born in the south, on a southern farm
I cut my teeth on the end of a hoe and have held
many plows in the crushes of my arm.

Many days I labored in heat from the scorching
sun
With little time for rest even less for having fun.

The summers were hot and the winters were cold.
But as a child, I did as I was told.

Whether the fields bore cotton, corn, or peas,
It had no reflection on the life I wanted for me.
After eighteen years of sweat and tears,
The age of accountability finally set me free.

To the empty pockets of the farmer' profession,
I've bowed in mind never to return.
To a greater calling in life I press toward the mark
in a world of uncertainties each day as I sojourn.

To stir up the spirit in men and women in this
deceitful world,
I'm determined somehow to find a way.

If God will give me strength and courage, and
guide the directions of my hands, feet, and mind,
The goal I seek, I'll find someday.

I refuse to sit down doing nothing when
something can be done.
If I never try, I know defeat will always be mines
And ways to succeed will always be none.

My strength and abilities are limited being alone
But with the help and approval of the eternal God,
My good and honorable deeds can prove to be
endless.
The scripture confirms, as a Christian, I wrestle
not against flesh and blood but against
principalities and powers stronger than I
And while alone, this battle I cannot win,
I have on my side a friend and Savior undefeatable
by all existing powers;
He overcame the trials and temptations of this
world and yet remained sinless.

When my enemies close doors before my face,
And high and unmovable walls block my path,
These things shall not make me go astray.
No wall is too thick or high for God to bring down;
Nor has there ever been a door closed that God
could not open;
When I humble myself in sincere prayer,

The way through, over, or around my enemies,
My God will surely show me the way.
As a child, often I drifted; while speaking to God in
secret places, tears ran steadily from my eyes.
As I was then, so am I now; tears still run down my
face whenever recurring sorrows arise.

In dreams and visions, I've been many things
But in reality, I'm only a man.
Quieter than some: more determined than others:
I'm a man with many skills nourished by the care
of my hands.

Like King David, I've been young and now I'm old;
I've seen things strange and witnessed things
essential for the Christian soul.

The hopes and dreams of many are being cut
short by the deeds of evil men and women.
The picture the news media paint through it
various sources, seem to indicate that in the race
between good and evil
Good is slowing down and falling behind
While evil seem to be gaining speed and soaring
like the wind.

Secret places and times in my life still exist
Talks with God are now more frequent
Not so much for me as for others

I've come to grip with what I am.
Reaffirming the words of the patriarch Job,
Things we regret the most will come to pass;
When feelings of entrapment rob me of hope,
It is then I solicit the strength and guidance of a
comforting Lamb.

With this gift that God has given to me,
I want to share it when, where, and however I
can.
The impact I desire to leave on the hearts of those
I touch,
Whether through spoken words, speech,
character, or written material,
Is to lead men, women, boys and girls, to confirm
without doubt
That James Earl Smith was truly a godly man.

Haiku of James Earl

My load gets heavy
Under pressure, I stumble
Faith keeps me going

Alive but alone
So often this has been me
Corralling my tears

Held captured by death
In spired by hateful words
I became victim

Trying to keep faith
Among evil demons wile
One day at a time

Embracing oneness
Favoritism I had none
Hurts were plentiful

My spirit warrant
The good we should see in all
Jesus Christ died for

Tears of long ago
Ever flowing in my veins
Lasting hurts return

In a childhood cage
Sentenced to shame and ruin
Unfairly from home

Dreading thirty-five
A joy taken in childhood
Condemned a life

Always left behind
Tears embraced loneliness
Memories return

Often put to shame
The God within was my shield
As laughter rang out

Lizzie With Husband JD (5th Sibling)

Lizzie Mae Smith was named after her grandmother on her father side. In the community of Coldwater Mississippi to the parents of Robert Lee and Lula Mae Smith, She was born on Jan. 1, 1951 and was the third Smith sibling to graduate from the Tate County High School as an honor student. Leaving high school in the spring of 1969, she went on to marry her high school sweet heart, J D Davis, and their first child was born in December of that same year. Seeking a better life for themselves, they moved to Detroit, Mi. in 1970. After living in Michigan for nearly 50 years, she says her mind sometimes reflects back to how Dorothy in the wizard of OZ must have felt being away from the place of her birth. Lizzie loved farm life and all the chores and togetherness that accompanied farm life. She was fascinated by the way her parents and other elderly relatives were able to cure any and all illnesses that occurred within the family using simple remedies found in nature. In a short period of two years, they were able to move into their own house before their second child was born in 1972. The West Side Church of Christ welcomed the family to the community and made them feel at home with warmth and harmony. Soon Lizzie got involved in Religious teaching and continues to love it today. Her third child was born in 1974 and they became a family of five. During the period between 1979 and 1981 she went through a stage of different illnesses and constantly taking medication kept her in a daze every day. Finally, she decided on her own to stop taking the medication and rely more on the God that had supplied her needs while on the farm and her health and life got better. She began during volunteer work in the school system and later in 1990 she was hired and worked for different schools as a cook, a task she loved and still loves today, this she did for the next twenty-two years before retiring. Lizzie and her husband, Jack, now have four children and seven grandchildren and have been married for almost forty-eight years. She daily acknowledges God for all his blessings; the God introduced to her and all her siblings by her mother while she lived down on the farm has become a source of strength in her life. Having brought her a mighty long way, she has learned how to lean and depend on him every single day.

Sprinting Liz

You're not just another Smith sibling;
You're a special holiday child.
From year to year, as the world celebrates the
incoming year,
Each one you witness gives you reasons to smile.

It's duly noted you're younger than I
And whereas my birthday arouses no eye brows
Without world attention, your' never go by.

Though a splendid cotton picker you were,
From that part of your life, I know you're proud to
be free.
I'm told you have great sprinting legs;
To this, two of your sisters will always agree.

They say if you and Jesse Owens were in a race
together - and a dog barked
Poor Jesse Owens wouldn't stand a chance.
In seconds, even at your shadow, he would only
get a glance.

Whereas we have never denied the potato roots,
the cow mature tea, parched corn, or the hill side
dirt, that we digested in the life from which we
came,

Nor can we separate ourselves from the
undeniable legacy of our name.

Looking back on those hot and sweaty days,
There're peaceful avenues and a closeness I wish
we could reclaim.
Though the snake infected houses with their tin
top roofs,
I have no regrets of those being dame.

With a birthday that's celebrated all over the
world,
It must sometimes make you feel like a queen.
On your future birthdays I hope the Lord will
continue to bless you,
As he has done in the sixty six you've already
seen.

Today, away from the farm, no cotton to pick, no
night pots to empty, or milk to churn before going
back to the field,
You're now living in the comforts of the city.
I'm not there nor do I pretend to know what city
life is like
But when we consider the crimes that are going
on around us
We can embrace the past without showing pity.

Whatever we are: whatever we've done:

Wherever we've been: wherever we're going:
We should never forget from whence we came.

There're memories in our past we may be
tempted to forget
But those memories helped to shape and make us
into what we are today;
They're roots in which none of us should ever be a
shame.

Haiku of Lizzie

With dogs on your heel
Squalling preceded the wind
Blood was left behind

A fowl in the hand
Drew a target for practice
Tears brought on regrets

By the grace of God,
On New Year a life was born
Faith keeps it growing

A name reclaimed
Passed down through legacy

Mother to grandchild

One was- then was not
A voice was heard disappeared
Sound outran dust

Needs take priority
Juggling home and motherhood
Rest is rarely found

Herbert Smith is the twelfth child of Robert and Lula Smith. Through birth he entered life on earth for a brief moment then was taken from this sinful world to dwell among the heavens where returned spirits dwell. Though his hands never touched neither cotton stalk nor plough, for nine long months, he too felt the stress and agony of life on the farm. He never saw or played with any of his elder siblings but like them, he was blessed to share the same dynamist mother. He was the last of his siblings to be born and the first to be called home by God. The incidents surrounding his birth inspired my first serious prayer. I, like all my siblings, had watched our mother down on her knees bended over a four legged wooden chair every night. We knew she was speaking to God through her prayers but we didn't know what she was saying. We observed her and showed respect during her time of communing with God. Our mother was always presence within our midst and supplied all our needs whether they were physical or spiritual but during the time of Herbert birth, May 30, 1961, she was not just away from home but in a hospital for the first time and it was a very scary moment. Fearing we might lose her, I went down on my knees and repeated not only the model prayer, which I said every night but I made a promise to God that if he would return her back home safe again then I would devote my life to him for as long as I lived. After nearly seven decades, I have never forgot that promise and I try to do the best I can to fulfill that promise. I don't know what memories mom carries in her heart concerning Herbert but I do know that she loved him like she do and have loved all of her children. She has never shown a different between any of us no matter how ungraceful some of us might have been to her. Today Herbert' spirit is in the heavens and the love of him will always remain in his siblings memories but in his mother heart.

Silent Hebert

As did we, from the same parents you came.
And our blood links us to the same name.

Those nieces and nephews you might have had
Will never have the opportunity to call you dad:

For nine months, your body saw no light
Now your spirit is surrounded by angels of light.

In God' care, where you now reside
Only God can be your guide.

You never knew us: we never knew you:
But we know of the God where your spirit went.
You were spared from the burdens of this sinful world
So to meet your God, you want have to repent.

The youngest child: the youngest boy:
The one we never had the chance to enjoy.

You've never felt the arms of your earthly mother
Nor walked hand and hand with your sisters or
brothers
But you'll always find comfort in your heavenly
father.

Haiku of Hebert

Never known or seen
Never forgotten in thought
That which was will be

Connected by blood
Life lives even after death
From the grave love speaks

Having never met
Living through many shared hearts
A name never dies

Ascended spirit
Last to be born first to die
Never forgotten

Life without a start
No yesterdays or today
But tomorrow waits

Part two

Poems of People, Events, Things, and Etc.

The Life of Belinda

The passing of Belinda brought us much sorrow
But the spirit of her love will greet our every tomorrow.

By offering her mind, feet, hands, and body, to aid those in
need,
Many were enlightened by her diver deeds.

To her church, town, school, and community,
She offered them her best.
No child of God would offer anything less.

With the mark that crowns a godly child,
Her greetings were always gentle and mild.

During the final minutes of her life here on earth, I'm told;
her mouth uttered no complaints.
From among us, her energetic spirit will never grow faint.

Though none of us wanted to see her go,
She's gone down a path that all the living must someday
follow.

Concerning her life, many spoke well
It seemed the whole community had something to tell.

Her children were the greatest source of her life
And to Witt, her soul mate, she was an inspiring wife.

Sometimes her words were not polite; but in delivering
them, never did she squirm.

On the grounds of her beliefs, she was one who stood
firm.
The character of Belinda, may we never forget
Though the passing of her life we'll always regret.

Much of the danger that comes our way in life, to change,
we have no voice
No one welcomes pains or sufferings in life by choice.

Many of the things that come into our lives without
request,
As she did, we too, we must learn to accept.

These things we may not want or desire to see
But they're frailties of life from which only death can set us
free.

To a spiritual dwelling place, Belinda has gone
There in peace she'll rest and never be alone

Someday the trumpet of God shall sound
And the dead shall rise from the sea and ground.

Perhaps we'll meet Belinda again at the time of the end.
Where, with our Lord, everlasting life, we'll spend.

There's this place in the heavens prepared for the saints
There the righteous will enter without complaint.

There'll be no more pains, deaths, or tears
And our days will have no ending years.

Thinking About You

It's been three years since we laid you to rest
And from time to time I still feel sad
A lot of things have happened since you passed
Both good things and bad
Around the time you left Donna and Keda became
pregnant
They named their babies Kamari and Brenaya
No doubt they were heaven sent
Two little angels who helped heal our hearts in a
way you wouldn't believe
They helped us accept the fact that God set you
free

I didn't cry at your funeral
And for a long time I felt guilty

Mom says people mourn in different ways
And I do it through my poetry

Been thinking about my future lately
Still not sure what I want to be
I just know I want to be happy in life
And have the whole family be proud of me

October 16, 2002
That's when the gates of Heaven opened up for
you to walk through
Although you're up in Paradise with Tupac, Biggie,
and Christ
We miss you like crazy and we love you too

I wish you could have watched me grow up
To have a career, some kids, and a wife
But instead of mourning your death
I'll just celebrate your life

Until we meet again
I'll stay strong and keep my head up
Since your spirit is with me in this cold world
I'll have the strength to never give up
Peace!!

By: Lamar Renfroe

A Picture's Epitaph

A picture displays countless imaginations
Things that could be or not be
The Fulfillment of a dream
An undeniable trophy

A beauty desired
But unreachable
A wishful love
But one that's untouchable

What we see
In words it does not speak
What it portrays
It has no control of

A mind soother
A heart breaker
Whether it's an image of beauty
Or one of disgrace

It can be a reminder of youth
And a revealer of old age
A composer of history not written in words
Yet displayed in countless imaginations

The Joy of Living

Life is a bundle of interest
We can build it up or tear it down
If we live a life of selfishness and evil,
It's bring shame on those we leave behind

Using our lives for the support of others,
Gain us a good name among our peers:
A title more precious than rubies or gold
That can only be earned through righteous living.

It'll speak for us whether we're presence or
absence
And a thief cannot destroy its image.
Enemies we're should to gain
But a friend we'll never lose.

Long after we're dead and gone
That we've gained will continue to live on.
A life has a way of inspiring other lives;
Every soul has something in this world to give.

Interest built up by the righteous will be
recompense with a crown in the world to come.
In the Lord, all that we've gained will not be loss
Knowing this will comfort us on our journey home.

January 6, 2017

Outside the ground was covered with snow
But there was warmth and comfort with us on the
inside.
The cold wind blasting against the windows
It constantly reminded us of the cold outside.

Friday morning, January 6
Brought in the first snow of the New Year
Schools and businesses were closed all around
And youths celebrated the day with laughter and
cheers.

For travelers going to and fro,

Highways were not a favorable friend
Ditches and hospitals had their fill
And countless fender benders saw no end.

Temperatures remained study in the teens.
Throughout the day no sunshine was seen.
In flight from trees to ground,
The birds searched but no food was found.

As light gave way to the coming darkness,
We beheld the day without animus.

From View of The Eyes

The craving of the eyes for things of beauty has
proven to be one of mankind's greatest
weaknesses.
If the beauty appears more than normal,
The heart will join in the pursuit

Though eyes and hearts may have an urge to
connect,
They may never venture into reality.
But when sight and feelings agree together
Accomplishments are always a possibility.

Extravagant

If both of us could mingle together in the same
pants,
We would create the sweetest musical chants.
Things said or done we may later recant
But for a brief moment the pleasures of our minds
and bodies would be enchant.

Remembering Horace Newson

A few days before Christmas 2016th, Horace
passed away;
Decreasing in numbers, the Tate County Hawks
are disappearing from history.
There's only a few of us left that can tell their
story.
Blue and gold were our colors
"Ole Tate County High, we hate to leave you" was
our song;
We left high school with dreams of fulfilling our
goals in a world of unlimited space.
As our days continue to increase in number, we
too will soon join up again with Horace.
Horace was one of us, a true Hawk, and he went
out from us

Though, it's been forty-nine years since I've seen
his face
The friendship we shared, time cannot erase.
Often we never get the chance to bid our
classmates farewell
But their memories - we'll keep and never sell.

The Richness of Being Black

Who am i?
I am a beautiful black woman in spite of what
others think.
Why am I black?
My God made me this way.
Should I feel lesser than other races?
I think not.
For I am a prestigious black woman,
Created in the image of the eternal God
Capable of being all God wants me to be
What I am
I'm proud to be.
For I am not a shame of being black,
In fact, I'm rather proud of this color of mines.
I've had it all of my life
And whether I'm dead or alive
I know it's a color that'll never change.

Unchangeable am I from birth to death
Real and unmistakably beautiful
I am the perfect symbol of peace and serenity
Like the darkness of the night
My inner thoughts are unsearchable.
I am the color that shows off the beauty of the
stars and moon in the night.
The world would be an unsettled place without
the Blackman and woman.
As black as night I might be,
But like all people God made me equal and free
Though many have tried to bring me down,
I'm a woman of color successfully holding my
own.
As long as my God is on my side,
An energetic Black woman, I'll continue to be.
I hope in my struggle to attain prosperity
I too will have the backing of the NAACP.

I Want To Hear

To tell me about the good I've done,
Don't wait till I'm gone.

If you have flowers to give,
Give them to me while I live.

When one is lying in the grave,
A voice of kindness cannot be heard.
While I live and have a nose to smell and eyes to
see,
Let me with my own two ears
Hear your kind devoted words.

Someone's Mother

Today, a mother is laid to rest;
The character thereof, we embrace this day
Her life displayed a strong faith
And a devotion given
Of a love unfeigned
Describing the life of a person
In mere words, one cannot say.
The fullness of her works is only known by the
heavens above
But those closest to her shared in the abundant of
her love.
You can see sadness on the faces of those she
held dear
But in their hearts, in memory, she'll always be
near.
For those we hold special in our hearts,
It's never easy to see them go.

The warmth and unselfish love this mother
inspired and taught
Those closest to her will never outgrow.
Maybe you knew her or perhaps you've heard of
her from a friend or other
This lady we're saying farewell too today
In deeds, she's proved to be someone' Mother.

Don't Let The Devil Steal Your Grace

God made man in his own image
And breathed into his nostrils the breath of life
All mankind breathe the same air,
Digest foods of diverse kinds,
Wear clothes of the same color and fashion,
Drives cars of different colors and shapes,
Own pets and flowers of the same breed and
species,
And while they show no difference of their love of
these things
They find it hard to love the color of a living soul.
God made the world and all therein and saw that
all he did was good.
If man has the right to love the people of his
choice,

His love and knowledge of the living God must be misunderstood.

Don't let the devil steal your grace.

Of the living God, no man has seen the face.

It maybe of the color you detest being closest to down here on earth

If so, the devil will welcome you in the pit of hell, far away from the eternal God;

Don't allow hatred, prejudice, and the likes, to rob you of the living God eternal grace.

The Tate County Hawks Taking Flight

The Flight of The Tate County Hawks

The Tate County Hawks were in full strength by the year of nineteen hundred and sixty one.

Embracing our newly built school fully equipped
with running water, electric lights and gas heating,
Our hearts were filled with appreciation and
unison.
At first, we were small in numbers yet stimulus
and eagerness inspired us to grow.
With classes ranging from the fifth to the twelfth
grades,
The new school, to us, was a blessing from God
more visible and beautiful than the rainbow.
From the east, west, north, and south, sections of
the county, we assembled without remorse.
Together we became a notifiable force.
Adding diver sports and activities to the agenda
each year,
We praised our faculty and we held them dear.
At first, our only sports were baseball and
basketball.
To that list, within a few short years they added,
ban, choir, and football.
Soon an empty trophy room became a symbol of
delight to look within.
Inside was displayed all the achievements of our
heroine.
Those who came alone behind us were able to
witness symbols of the school' pride;
They too were inspired to follow the formal
Hawks in their stride.

In nineteen hundred and sixty six, we became the
district champions in football.
Being number one, we felt kind of tall.
With a magic in spirit that showed in our stroll,
Proudly we wore our colors of blue and gold.
The first group of Hawks flew from the nest prior
to nineteen hundred and sixty two
By nineteen hundred and seventy one, the name
of the hawks and their colors had been taken from
public view.
They took away the name and colors of the Hawks
of Tate County High;
But in the hearts of those who shares the name,
the fame of the Hawks will never die.

Soother

You come around more often than not
But never do or say a lot.
Your attendance is well and highly noted
But are your intentions pure devoted

This They Say

This they say:
When Jacob died,
Egyptians came to Canaan to mourn.

This they say:
When Goliath died,
Many people were there to see.

This they say:
When Jesus died,
His loved ones around the cross did mourn.

This they say:
When Martin Luther King died,
They came from near and far to mourn and see.

When you and I die,
Simple people we may be
But someone is sure to come and see.

I wonder.
What will they say?

Documented Truths

On the day of a person funeral
Swelling words are sure to be heard:
Whether they're true
Whether they're false
The dead will not return to life.

Hand and hand people may join
Whether they're men
Whether they're women
Today, either can be considered a wife.

Every human was given a mind
Whether it's used for good or evil:
The idle words said in secret
The hostile words said in anger
An account of them must someday be given.

Every life has an effect on one of another
Whether it produces a positive or negative effect:
We can choose to live life as we please
Or choose to live according to God' word;
Either way, we'll constantly be viewed by eyes
from heaven.

Coming To Grips With Reality

Ignorant is a growing phenomenon
In churches and governments, you can always find
its existence there.

People' desire to be seen in the spot light
Cause their ego to flare.

In authorities where ignorant rules,
Growth and prosperity will never succeed;
Known ignorant is a plus
For it knows its place.

Unknown ignorant has a defect;
It's blinded to its disgrace.

Knowledge is a key to dissolving ignorant
But ignorant must be willing to listen.

For truth to be accepted in any man' life,
His will to follow it must override his desire to
glisten.

Some Haiku

In an adult mind,
When childish desires take root
Truth is discorded

The heart prompts anger
Weapons of vast destruction
Need an igniter

On the Christian path,
Truth and good deeds show the way
As the spirit leads

Choices we all make
Choosing is mankind free will
Their worth, God shall judge.

Nothing is hidden
Silent speaks even in death
Unknowns are made known

On the day of death
Identifying the dead
Memories surface

The way of knowledge
In God there exist a way
To fulfill all things

Delusion

Long I've waited to taste the sweetness of your
lips.
Gentle hugs, friendly smiles, and soft spoken
words whispered in the ear can cause the
strongest man' faith to slip.
Dreams I've had; dreams I continue to have
concerning you.
With the what if's, and may be' constantly
questioning my reasoning,
I wrestle with what I should or should not do.
One gentle kiss from your lips to mines
This is what I truly crave.
But will it bring peace to a lonely heart
Or make of me your private slave?

Love Surface In Unknown Places

Friendships rarely turn into love affairs
But there're occasions they do flare.
Strange things have been known to happen
between friends without intent

But for a love affair to thrive both parties must consent.

Pains

While they're invaders of the body,
They show no preference of age or gender
One may have to digest various drugs as a suitable contender.
Some pains are self-inflicted: some are not:
Sometimes they're gentle and mild: other times they may hurt quite a lot.
Stock your medical cabinet with pills, antiseptic and patches or whatever you need to ease the pain.
Saying O! O My! Or some nasty word of profanity
Will serve no purpose nor would it help for you to complain.
From head to toe, they've been known to appear
And from time to time they'll fill your eyes with tears.
In children pain may cause them to cry till they're suffering for breath
But the aged are somewhat different; constant pains may cause them to long for the day of death.
Pains are not our friends or foe

Though they may be aftermaths of the things we sow.
The human body that's immune to hurts and pain
You'll find it resting out in death domain.

Reality

At funerals, tears are often shed
Expressing love toward one loved and dear;
Just as we long for the pleasures of life,
We must also prepare ourselves for the day of drear.
From the confinement of our mother womb, we entered life at birth.
Destine to someday return to a confinement within the heart of the earth.
As the death angels creep,
Many eyes will weep.
As sure as the life we come to know,
When we leave this world,
By way of death, we're sure to go.

If Minds Were Readable

If minds were readable,
Our inner most thoughts would be accessible.
What you know; I would know.
Fear would accompany us everywhere we go.
With no way of hiding our secret thoughts,
The resources of our mind would not be in doubt.

The Master's Choice

As black people, we know and speak of elements
that cause us to be failures.
If we examine those elements, we'll see many of
us have been labeled as users.
Jealousy, envy, and pride, are three of our main
foes.
Countless generations have failed to let them go.
Knowing of and what to do serve no purpose
We cannot move forward if we're unwilling to act.
Without giving up what brands us as Failures,
The unity of prosperity we'll never reach;
This is an undeniable fact.
Created equally in the image of God,
All men and women have potentials to grow.

Much like children, Adults growth can also be
halted by weaknesses in life they too need to
outgrow.
Being different in color is not a disgrace nor curse,
All that God made he declared it to be good
In nothing did he see any reason to reverse.
At the time the God head decided to make man,
They did it when and in their own way.
Whether we were made black, white, yellow, red,
or brown,
We all have reasons to be thankful each day.

Man's Earthly Trials And Journey

Into a world of unknown light every man comes
unaware of the darkness he must face on his way
out.
By trying to understand the ways of this simple
world,
He encounters situations unjust and devout.
The first man and his mate were told to be fruitful
and multiply
On an earth they were also told to subdue.
Every direction, every hill and mountain, were
within their power and freedom to pursue.
As man ventured out whether near or far,

Alone the way, he planted his seed.
All around the world men of every nation are at odds with each other
But from time to time they've found common grounds where they agreed.
Though mortal men sometime find common grounds upon which they can agree,
It is not within their human nature to ever be as one.
Only through the Son of God will they ever find unison.
From the beginning, God said it was not good for man to be alone;
Today, there're millions of men upon earth
But their most difficult task is finding ways to get alone.
Man born of a woman, if he lives to be threescore and ten
In that allotted time, can he live a life free of sin?
He was stronger by himself without the bones of his bones
His weakest moment seems to have come when he joined with his wife and the two became as one.
Disappointing his God by eating the forbidden fruit,
Each time the living God is denied, it leaves one vulnerable for Satan to recruit.
It is appointed once for every man to die.

This is a destiny to which we all must comply.
From the first man Adam, we inherited sweat and tears.
Before the second man Adam, we must someday all appear.
The curse of death, we owe to the first man and his wife.
But it is to the second man Adam we owe the greatest gift of all----------Eternal Life.

Thinking of Lavern

He was laid to rest in his favorite color of clothes
Surrounding his casket was a bright selection of red roses.

Many came to witness the passing of Bro. Lavern Rowell.
They came by two's three's and even four's to say their farewells.

Above three scores and ten, he was a resident of this earth.
Much of that time was spent in the home where his four Sons were given birth.

A man of few words, he was known to be.
Now, his body is free of pains and his spirit is in harmony.

A family man and husband to Winonia
That stayed by her side till death took him away.
Though, it's not for him but for the living we should take time to pray.
As the family assembled to say their last good – byes,
Tears were presence within their eyes.

In this ceremony, many refer to as a wait,
It is not one anyone cares to celebrate.

Within our neighborhood, he was the eldest
And of those called home, he was the latest.

Winonia was his only known soul mate
Their love, not even death was able to terminate.

Now that he's gone home and left Winonia alone
Many of nights, her heart will surely groan.

In the heart of Winonia, will family and friends be able to ward off loneliness?
Will memories of Lavern be enough to maintain her happiness?

Though questions we may ask,
Only Winonia will know how she feels
But whatever her needs
Whatever the hurts
In the process of time
Them
The God of the heaven will surely heal.

Though Silent, Death Speaks

To look upon the dead today,
Is to see ourselves in a day to come;
To look upon one who is dead,
Arouses our knowledge of returning home;
When God recalls the breath of life,
Man must return to his place of origin.
If man fall to sleep in the Lord,
Someday, he'll be called to rise again.
Without the spirit of life given by God,
The body is only an empty shell.
We may question the dead' reasons for leaving
But there is nothing the dead can say or tell.
Death gets our attention like nothing else
While it reminiscence things of our formal days.
As long as blood runs freely through our veins,

If need be, we still have the chance to change our ways.
Witnessing the face of the dead
Gives us a view of what we'll someday be.
By choice, this end is not our' to make;
It's a warrant handed down by heaven decree.

I Didn't Know

I didn't know;
I had no knowledge of the day of your passing.
While I wrestle with the pain of missing you,
I'm left in a state of remorse and mourning.
Had I known of your untimely death
I would have rallied to give comfort to those you
hold most dear.
By your side, I too would have wanted to be near.
We grew up together.
Your parents and mines were close to each other.
You knew of me; I knew of you.
Your death deeply saddened me when I got the
news.
Someday, like all others, I'll leave too
And come to the place where you have gone.
People are leaving this world every day;
In it, we live; but it is not our own.

We had no say when we entered herein
And have no rights to choose when it's time to go.
Death is the door way out of this life
And the entry way into the next:
What you've done I'm well aware of;
When you did it bewildered me,
I would have definitely bade you a final farewell
But
"I didn't know."

Coming To Grips With Life

At birth, the womb opens up to let living flesh out;
At death, the earth opens up to take it in.

We enter this world without a fault
But leaving it we cannot escape the death of sin.

A child looks forward to days of play;
Adults seek ways of making every day pay.

Worries are not the concern of youths;
They're reserved for their latter days.

What we accumulate in life is our to use as long as
we live;

But at life' end, all that we have, to another we must give.

To die is the only true thing in this world that every man must do.
To the living, the sight of death is nothing new.

In our sojourn through life we're privileged to
A few days of trouble and few days of pleasure;
One or both are bound to be sure.

Under The Moon Light

With only the moon light visible in the sky,
Walking up and down the roadway
It was the only light on which I had to rely.
While silence reigned, darkness surrounded me.
Even the movement of my feet I was unable to see.
I could hear the sound of predators chasing their prey
Ready to devour everything eatable in their pathway:
The moon preceded and followed me alone the road as I went.

It being in my presence, I could not resent.
The nearer I came to the morning' dawn,
The completion of my walk kept winding down.
There's a silence I heard at the beginning of my walk
It stopped when the woodlands filled up with bird chatter and talk.
In the morning commute, passing motorists in their flight,
Rarely took the time to be polite.
Ending my journey prior to twilight
I went into the house and immediately nourished my appetite.

The Tate County Hawks In Their Descent

A Poetic Epitaph of The Falling Hawks

They left the nest at an early age in search of
dreams their parents were denied.

A driving urge within their soul drove them toward a freedom the black man had always desired.

The honor of graduation had made their parents proud.
And in their generation, they were determine to see the black man' potentials un- shroud.

They took their leave from their home nesting grounds by means of trains, cars, ships, planes, and some even on feet
As they ventured out to challenge the unknown;
They entered a new frontier with only determination as their chaperone.

On the list of falling hawks, you'll find the names of Smith, Jackson, Todd, Milton, Boyd, Hawkins, Leisure, Robinsons, Cummins, White, Turner, Mallory, and Brown, just to name a few.
And on my long list of remembrance there are still others that I also knew.

Thus far, the Hawks have survived above five decades
But sadly year by year, we're declining in number.

The football, basketball, ban, choir, and various competitions we engaged in while we were in school gave us satisfactions above measure;
It's those inspiring connections I'll always remember.

The six week tests, report cards, laughter, tears, lunch hours, and childhood friendships, are personal relics of the declining Hawks history.
Though they're things and events of our distant past,
I'll always keep them stored in my memory.

Some of the migrating nesting grounds of the Hawks can be found in Tennessee, Missouri, Michigan, Washington D.C, and Oklahoma,
From year to year, many return home to their Mississippi birth grounds unknowing it for the last time.
Unlike their neighboring cousins, The Warriors, Cougars, Wildcats, and Mustangs, that's constantly ascending in numbers,
The Hawks are declining each year with fewer less mountains left to climb.

Special Qualities

Look at you;
You have a smile so delightful.

Every eye that focus upon you can see
From head to toe, you've been blessed bountiful.

When I look at you,
I can see nothing one would find to be shameful.

The one that shares your hand in marriage
Could not have found another so wonderful.

Anyone that looks upon you
To deny your beauty would be deceitful.

At home and work,
You're faithful and dutiful.

Well you were taught;
Your devotion to God is never wasteful.

You show through the example you set
In Christ, you strive in every known way to be
useful.

Being friend to you is truly an honor,
Having that privilege, I will always be graceful.

Violent Crimes

Why are they rising?
Why are they raging?

In homes, schools, churches, department stores,
banks, gas stations, you name it; they're there.
In every other section of the country, they're
battling crimes just like we are here.

Young people, old people, men, women, educated
and non-educated, governments, churches, from
either group they've been known to rise.
These days it's hard to determine who's good or
evil before they make themselves known before
our eyes.

Crimes are rarely hidden like they once were.
Today' perpetrators show no fear.

They're not frighten by police or jail
Putting their lives in harm' way, they seem to have
little concern as to whether they succeed or fail.

Work is said to be a profession that's honorable in
all
Yet few today follow that path

Today, to attain their needs, the evil hearted
would rather steal and brawl.

As long as people keep giving in to sin,
Heaven gates will never open to let them in.

The Power Within And Above

Though they weigh heavy on our soul,
Some words are better left untold.

If it keeps others confident from being broken,
The truth is sometimes best unspoken.

Our faith helps to coral feelings the heart admits.
Things we desire the most is sometimes off limit.

When we're slipping in and out of sin,
And struggling to maintain our faithfulness,
It's good to have at our disposal a God that offers
forgiveness.

The Brightest Light of All

This morning I saw a long star
Brightly shinning in the east;
It reminded me of a star of long ago
That led the wise men on their quest.

Looking down on me from a distant high
It showed off a glitter of sparkling light
I wondered as I walked along the road side
Why there was no moon or other stars in sight.

Up there in the sky, though alone it was,
It did what stars are bound to do.
As it caught my attention,
It puzzled me in thought and view.

Then, I was reminded of the ancient of days gone
and those to come;
In the days of old, it only took one star to guide
the ships alone the water ways at night.
For us, there is only one Son in the heaven
His radiant out shines the brightest star
And through the spiritual darkness of this world
Only he can lead us into the marvelous light.

Life's Norms

No two fruits look or taste the same
Nor is every actor destine for fame.

A man' life entails gratitude and shame
Though the latter he would rather not claim.

Formed by grace and erected with a human
frame.
A living soul man became.

Within a man heart there a yearning that ignites a
flame
One only love has been able to tame.

The deeds we sow in life produce effects we
cannot disclaim.
That we sow we shall also reap; this the Holy
Scriptures proclaim.

Nicknames are substitutes for our given names
And carries with them no guilt or blame.

One who lives may never attain the fullness of his
aims
But life itself, he can acclaim.

Fragrance

In the early spring mornings,
The sweetness of the honey suckers fills the air.
Hanging thick on tree branches and fence lines,
Their blossoms let off an admirable flair.

The yellow and white coloring attracts the
mocking bird to the scent of their sweetness.
Even human have been known to affirm their
taste-ness.

Dripping with dew drops in the morning sun light
Passer buyers have been known to stop and take a
bite.

It Works For Me

Under a full moon with freshness in the air,
Under darken skies, in my walks I find solitaire.
Listening to the voice of the early birds before
sunrise,
I find; it's an ideal time to take my daily exercise.

Un-reversible

When a man dies,
It is said he goes to a better place.
When a body is taken from among this sinful
world,
We're told the spirit finds peace within God grace.

Whether the dead enjoys more contentment than
the living,
Only one that has returned from the grave can
truly tell.
The living rarely has a desire to go to the place of
the dead, especially when all is going well.

Many things tradition teaches us to say and do
And although we say and do them
We're clueless to the reason why.
After experiencing the joys and gifts of this life,
We become attached to the things of this world
So, it's not an easy thing to say good-bye.

Every day through the media death is flashed
before our face.
Knowing any day our time could come,
Whether it's to a better place or worse,
With death and the grave we know,
We must all someday interlace.

Under Surveillance

Today, a rabbit came out of the thicket to observe
me as I strolled up and down the road.
He seemed more curious than fearful as he sat on
his two hind legs occasionally hoping from time to
time like a summer' toad.
Back and forward, up and down the road I went
But with my presence, he seemed content.
Up above our heads the stars stood on their post
While me and the rabbit to one another served as
host.
To me, the rabbit spoke neither a word.
To him from me, not one was heard.
Soon, he ceased watching me.
There must have been greater things he wanted
to see.
Hoping away like a popinjay,
The rabbit went on his merry way

Note Worthy

Feminine growth in all the proper places,
Has been known to arouse minds and attract the
focus of many faces.

Resources

What your heart needs to feel from time to time
My eyes love to see knowing it can never be
mines.
One never gets enough of the softness of your
touch.
Dreams are created by such.
In the wisdom issued through the opening of your
lips,
One can find comfort in the smallest sip.
Undeniable are all your credentials
They're living evident of your greatest potentials.

Forever Missed

Taking in by your elaborate charm
In visions, I've held you in my arms
Often, your love I've wanted to claim
But to do so would brand each of us with shame.
With a decade between us catching up is not an
option,
You'll always remind me of the one that never
was who got away.
This in word and thought is my secret re su-me'.

Love Is Terminal

Love is a worthy companion
It'll carry you far
Befriend you long
But never deceives you
To please another

To My Siblings

Where love is envy' presence cannot enter
Such an atmosphere one should seek to crave.

Knowing peace and harmony dwell within its
midst
Bear reasons for one to acquire and save.

There was a spirit planted in our lives in the past
That gave us the will to survive.
The living Lord was that source and in him and
through him daily we live.

Yes, we were limited to certain areas around town
and endured many other unwanted and unjust
hardships with invisible walls.
Life on the farm was calm and peaceful
But none of us have ever confessed to it being an
inaugural ball.

I remember the country gardens, the berries
thickets, grape vines, and black walnut trees.
In the summer times, from these, to partake of
their produce, we were free.

It was the long hot sweaty days of farm life
That prepared and shaped us for our future
callings.
Even though today none of us live on a farm,
We will never forget it was our beginning.

From a long standing single profession,
Our families grew.

Each generation seem to have ventured into one
that is new.

By our mother' example, cleaving to the Lord at a
very young age,
We came to realize that all things are possible if
we only believe.
Many times, we may feel that we're all alone and
various trials and tribulations may come our' way,
But we have the assurance of our Lord' word that
from our presence, he'll never leave.

The majority of our school terms were spent
mainly in the cotton fields
But our knowledge exceeded many that attended
every day.
School records will confirm this to be true
Starting with Robert Earl and myself down to
Brother Jimmy, of this, you'll find no misleading
hearsay.

Parents taught us to obey the laws of the land.
By example, we too, must teach our children with
a firm hand.

The same God that took us and our parents from
behind the plough
Someday, before him we all must bow.
Life is not only comprised of work and play

There're times when we must also take time to pray.

Some of us today have different last names and live in separate households
But our linkage can be traced back to the same mold.

And who can forget those glorious memories of childhood, the long summer days that seemed to have no end, whether we were in the fields, engaged in diver kinds of games or just running up and down the road and pastures loving every available minute of laughter and play?
At night we could hear the hooting of the old wise owl, probing the woodlands in search of prey.

The bond of faith that parents, children, relatives, and friends shared in those bygone days of our childhood is in jeopardy today of being misunderstood.
Love is the bond that kept and keeps us
Together; love supplies the kindness that helps us to forgive and get alone with others in spite of our differences; love is a virtue that was and is shared with the world by a God that we know the scripture declares to be good.

We cannot return to the ere of our childhood

Nor would we readily give up the blessings that God has blessed us with thus far.
To the eternal God, we owe the richness of our past, the security of our present, and the hope of our future, his brightness supersedes the morning star.

Though we're all grown up today, the child in us ever lives.
Every time we're feeling down and out, when we reminiscence the past, it gives us the strength to revive.

A Tribute To Pastor Jessie L. Barber

To your tenure, forty-seven years you have to claim.
For those years, the following contributions overshadow your name.

J – is for **Jesus**; embracing the young, feeding the hungry, remembering the poor, certifies your credentials as an ambassador of Jesus

E – is for **Exquisite**; you have shown exquisite dedication for the well beings of the members of William Memorial Baptist Church

S - is for **Service**; whenever needs arose, you
   fulfilled your obligations day and night

S - is for **Successfully**; you've led this church
   successfully for forty-seven graceful years

I - is for **Inspired**; with stern and inspired truths,
   you have promoted our Christian growth.

E - is for **Everyone**; your leadership has touch the
   heart of everyone within your flock

L – is for **Love**; I am overwhelmed by the love
   you've shown all the member of this church

E –is for **Exceptional;** we've been honored by your
   exceptional preaching of God' inspired words

E - is for **Expectations**; you've fulfilled our
   greatest spiritual desires and expectations

B – is for **Belief**; your hospitality has furthered our
   belief in the eternal living God

A –is for **Assurance**; your assurance has given us
   faith in the risen Lord

R –is for **Rest**; from the toils of your labor, you've
   earned the rights to rest

B -is for **Brother**; you've been a faithful brother
   and pastor that have watched over us through
   our trials and tribulations

E –is for **Eternally**; for you, we shall always be
   eternally graceful

R –is for **Remembered**; your faithful service to us
   will be forever remembered

During your tenure, like **Jesus**, your **exquisite service successfully inspired everyone** with **love** and **exceptional expectations.** In your **belief** and **assurance** of your self-sacrifices, be of good cheer. While you take your **rest,** as a faithful **Brother** of the gospel, know that you'll be **eternally remembered.**

Calm

I found a picture of you in my desk drawer
Unblemished by age, you still look the same.
Above your forehead a little gray shows,
With nothing gain, nothing loss, perfection is
within your frame.

With an illuminating spirit,
To you, others are drawn.
In your footsteps,
They wish to follow where you have gone.

Leadership qualities
You possess.
Your appearance, stature, and wisdom
You've maintained well without duress.

Love's Connection

Love is a four letter word
It cures **L**oneliness
Overrides prejudice
Varies from heart to heart
And sometime **E**scalates to be absurd:

Mattie

When I finally met you,
It was many years too late
Another had claimed your heart
And sealed your eligibility' fate.

When I observe the magnitude of your smile,
It sends blood rushing through my veins.
I wrestle daily with right and wrongs
As I try faithfully to stay above the dividing line.

When I have the pleasure of greeting you
Wishful thoughts emerge before I let you go.
If eyes could only talk,
There would be no end to what ears would know.

When I'm near you,
I feel all warm inside.
Yet what my heart feels
I try diligently to hide.

The sight of you each week
Always inspires my heart.
I always feel a sense of misery when
It comes time for us to depart.

The Poet's Specialty

What inspires the poet' pen?
Sight and sound
Every voice
Every smile
Tear drops
Embrace
Whether friend' or lover'
When rhythms flow,
Poets give them knowledge to grow.

Preacher Man

Your words
Stepping stones
Stumbling blocks
They build up
Tears down
Encourages
And rebukes
What others heed
Do you concede?

A Ballad of John Boyd Sr.

With his children all grown up and out on their own,
Apart from Mother Bell, John Sr. found himself all alone.

The quite nights brought him no peace
Neither did association with people at the local Walmart give him ease.

Alone, without his soul mate

Many nights the midnight oil was burned late.

Missing the company of his wife of many years,
In equal comparison, nothing in this world could
ever cohere.

Joined are the souls of a husband and wife
When one departs, the other soon yearn the
presence of the afterlife.

Making preparation to enter into the marvelous
light,
As sickness entered his body, he found no will to
fight.

In what the world had to offer, he no longer found
pleasure
Rather he chose to enter the heaven where lies
his greatest treasure.

In life, when loneliness continues to increase
Being alone, the will to live continues to decrease.

With a life span that stretches above four-scores
and ten,
His life span was one that has only been shared by
few modern men.

There's a notable line between birth and death

It begins with life and ends when death takes away our final breath.

To say farewell is not the easiest thing for loved ones to say,
If it was possible, with us, they would gladly stay.

A few years ago, Mother Bell was called home
But today, June 10, 2017, was unforeseen as the day that John' Sr. call would come.

The death of John has left tears in the eyes of those he loves
But hopefully they'll find comfort in knowing he has found joy and peace in the presence of the heavens above.

The eternal God has blessed us with a mind to reminiscence and embrace the lives of our loved ones memories.
They're thoughtful reminders to uplift our spirit when we're drowning in miseries.

The spirit of John Sr. has left the earth and ascended into the sky
But he left his loved ones in the hand of a God in whom they can always rely.

Secure

There were many knights around King Author'
table.
By their wisdom and strength, the land was kept
stable.
There's only two hearts that bind us together
But the bond created helps us survive the storms
of life in all sorts of weather.

A Grave Side Eulogy

To you, I gave my love.
To my nation, I gave my mate.
In return, you gave me loneliness.
In your honor, my nation gave me a flag.

What I gave to you, you kept.
What I gave to my nation, they buried.
While I face the future on my own,
I'm left with much to moan.

Keeping It Real

Where love never ends,
Hurt never begins.
When truth rules the day,
Lies are cast away.
Where a house is made a home,
It allows prosperity to come.
Whenever people find themselves in diver needs,
A Good Samaritan intercedes.
When a repentance sinner is forgiven,
The offer of salvation is given.

Feasting In Danger

Road Kill
In groves, vultures gather to feast.
They rid the roadside of deaths from large to
least.
The only fear they have of enjoying a taste meal
Is the threat they face from speeding
Automobiles.

A Watchful Eye

If you knew how often I focus my eyes upon you,
With me, you would properly have an uneasy
issue.
With style and elegance in the performance of
your duty,
While you are my friend, I cannot deny your
overwhelming beauty.
From the hair on your head to the dividing of your
toes,
Everything about you, I'm intrigued to know.
I notice; I notice; even when you're not unaware.
In you, I see; a woman with qualities that are rare.

To Be With You

What would I not give or
Where would I not travel to be with you?
The best of my days and nights to come,
The death of loneliness and birth of happiness,
These I would have a chance to discover, if you
allow me, to be with you.

The dreams of my childhood, the warmth of friendship,
Fuel the need to be with you.
With hugs and kisses, I would whisper gentle word
into your ears telling you of my desires to be with you.
All of my love would be your to explore;
While I caress the softness of your breasts
And nibble on the sweetest of your lips
Grant me opportunity- to be with you.

Unavoidable

Whether we believe or whether we not
The truth is "we must all someday die"
Death is a reappearing occurrence that
We cannot avoid or deny.

Growing Up

When I was in Kindergarten, I learned a lot of stuff.
Like counting, coloring, and it was really tough.

In first grade, I learned how to write and also how to fly a kite.

In second grade, I was able to add and subtract; I thought I would never learn to do that.

In third grade, multiplying was really tough but then it got easy and I couldn't get enough.

In fourth grade, my teacher was so kind I could always tell what was on her mind.

In fifth grade, everything was sort of easy; the teachers gave us plenty to keep us busy.

This year I've learned and enjoyed a lot; boy those teachers can put you on the spot.

I've really enjoyed elementary school and all the things I've done.

Now I'm going to the 7th grade –High School --- here I come!

Written by Sandra Smith

Undeniable

The girl that sat beside me
Like the one that sat in front
Caught the attention of my eye:
Focusing upon these two
My eyes saw pleasures that
My mind could not deny.

At Day's End

With a combination of pleasures and sorrows,
We look forward each day to a tomorrow.
What we're unable to do today
Tomorrow gives us a chance to find a way.
When our final today set us free,
All of our tomorrows will cease to be.
The grave shall open up to take in its prey.
While there – neither man nor beast shall ever
stray.

Catastrophes of Life

Where men and women together dwell
There lust will eventually rise.

When beauty catches the attention of the eye,
Heart beats are sure to react.

When parties of the object sex embrace
Wishful desires come into thought.

A thousand years of togetherness
Cannot erase the hurt of deceit:

Where walls are built to sustain lies
A day of truth shall cause them to scatter.

To secure and keep the heart of a desirable lover,
One must put away the dark things of the past.

Where vows are made between two or three
Devotion from all parties will be required.

Reality and truth can inspire a relationship
But only the **Gift** of God can make it work.

Angelical

This pain in my heart
Steadily, it aches for you.
To share a moment of your love,
It's my dream one day to do.

Unknown

When time comes to part this life,
Bags packed or not
To the grave, it's our destiny to go.
All said and done on that day
It will not arouse our interest to speak;
Being dead, we'll never know.

Our God Cares

Every day, we find something to complaint about.
If it's not the rain, we target the drought.
We serve a God that knows better than we.
To supply our needs, we have his personal
guarantee.

About The Author

This author is a lover of poetry and religion. To date, I have written twelve books outlining my love for poetry as well as truths concerning God word. In an effort to reach the hearts of mankind, I search for words of inspiration that will uplift the spirit of men and women in their presence condition. As God continues to bless me, I shall continue to write. Hoping and trusting that someone will find solace in the pages of my words.

www.ingramcontent.com/pod-product-compliance
Lightning Source LLC
Chambersburg PA
CBHW060757050426
42449CB00008B/1439